BOY, YOU ARE BRILLIANT!

ASHLEY AYA FERGUSON

ILLUSTRATED BY: LEE EDMOND JOHNSON

For my dear brother Joe, who taught me how to free myself with honesty, vulnerability and authenticity. This book is also dedicated to my dad and brother Shawn who set great examples of what it means to be brilliant.

You sir, are *BRILLIANT!*
You *SHINE* just like a star,
You can do anything!
Do you know *WHO YOU ARE?*

What does it mean to be *BRILLIANT?*
It means intelligent, set apart —
A WONDER OF THE UNIVERSE.
You can do amazing things,
If you *BELIEVE* in yourself first.

When it's dark and scary in the world,
You are **WARM AND BRIGHT**,
Even if no one told you —
YOU ARE IMPORTANT!
Someone out there needs your **LIGHT**.

Do you believe it?
Say, *"I AM BRILLIANT!"*
And, don't be ashamed of
what you know,
Following the crowd is boring,
Let's see how far *YOU* can go.

Being strong and tough is cool,
But it's *NOT ALL* that you are.
Everybody hurts sometimes.
SHOW CARE when it's not you
that's down, it won't dim *YOUR STAR.*

Sometimes, you might have
to help a friend, and you should —
DON'T LEAVE OTHERS BEHIND!
It feels good to be good to people,
You can **BE STRONG** and you can
BE KIND.

You sir - are *BRILLIANT!*
Don't be afraid to *SPEAK UP*
and *SHINE YOUR LIGHT.*
The world is better with you in it,
Something you do could *SAVE A LIFE!*

People will doubt your *BRILLIANCE*,
Some don't want to see you *SHINE*,
That's even more of a reason to show them,
How *GREAT* you are time after time.

You can *STAND TALL,*
and reach high heights,
You can move fast, and *GO FAR.*
But, don't forget to
LIFT UP OTHERS as you rise,
TEAMING UP with brilliant
ones enhances who you are.

You, my friend, are *BRILLIANT,*
BRIGHT AND AMAZING all by yourself
Still - don't ever be afraid,
in times of need to use your words
and seek out those who can *HELP.*

When you talk people listen,
You have **POWER** inside of you!
Nothing can take away
your **BRILLIANCE** —
If there are obstacles,
you can **BREAK THROUGH**.

You sir, are **BRILLIANT,**
Resilient, joyous and true,
Don't be afraid to smile,
IT LOOKS GOOD ON YOU.

ABOUT THE AUTHOR

Ashley Ferguson is the author of Girl, You Are Magic! and Boy, You Are Brilliant! When she is not writing, she spends time with her daughter, Nia, and speaks to students about the power of words. Most of the time; however, she is reading, writing or talking about reading and writing.

www.ingramcontent.com/pod-product-compliance
Lightning Source LLC
Chambersburg PA
CBHW040245100426
42811CB00011B/1151